A Study on the Holy Ghost

Rev. David D. Wilson

PARADISE GOSPEL PRESS

A STUDY ON THE HOLY GHOST, Wilson, David D.

First Edition

PARADISE GOSPEL PRESS

www.paradisegospelpress.com

ISBN: 978-1-946823-00-7

Introduction

In the church today, there's a misunderstanding about the Holy Ghost. People need to know who and what the Holy Ghost truly is, and what He does in the lives of believers. The church sets the Holy Ghost aside as if He's not important in our lives. It's time we understand the rightful place of the Holy Ghost in the church. Salvation comes through the shed blood of Jesus Christ. It's a gift from God, a way to bring us back into fellowship with God, as Jesus comes to live in our hearts and lives. As precious and wonderful as Jesus is, He's now in heaven with His Father. However, He hasn't left us alone. He has sent us another comforter, which is the Holy Ghost.

In putting together this Bible study, I want to impress upon people the importance of the Holy Ghost. People need to know who the Holy Ghost is and what part He plays in the plan of God. My primary source is Rev. Ralph M. Riggs' book, *The*

Spirit Himself. I consider Bro. Riggs' book to be the best book on the Holy Ghost I have ever read.

I also used *Matthew Henry's Commentary on the Whole Bible*, the *Dake Reference Bible*, *Barnes' Notes on the New Testament*, *What the Bible Says About the Holy Spirit* and the *Thompson Chain Reference Bible*. The comments in this study are mine, although the format mimics *The Spirit Himself.* I most heartily recommend that everyone read and study *The Spirit Himself.* I consider it a masterpiece; truly, Rev. Riggs was greatly used of the Lord.

The purpose of this study is to open people's minds to who the Holy Ghost is and what He can do in their lives. Most people think of the Holy Ghost as a second-class citizen in the Bible. They don't realize the Holy Ghost is the promised comforter Jesus said He would send to us after He went away. The part the Holy Ghost plays in our lives is that of keeper and protector. He leads us into the deep things of God. His job is to comfort us, to encourage us, and to lead us in the right way till Jesus returns for His Bride.

I pray this Bible study will enlighten you to what Jesus has given us in the Holy Ghost. May the Lord open and widen your understanding of spiritual things, and I hope this study does that for you. The Bible teaches us we are to study the word of God to show that we are striving to be what the Lord wants us to be.

Bro. David D. Wilson

The Holy Ghost

Who is He?
What is He?
What does He do?
How does He affect our lives?

As I study scripture, it's my belief that no one can be a consistent believer of the Bible without holding to the doctrine of the tri-unity of the Godhead. 1 John 5:7 states:

For there are three that bear record in heaven, the Father, the Word, and the Holy Ghost: and these three are one.

Note: In this study, all scripture is quoted from the *King James Version* unless otherwise stated. All scriptures are italicized.

These are three separate individuals with one purpose, one goal in mind: to reach a lost mankind; to give them a chance to receive salvation and join in fellowship with God. We were created for this fellowship with God but foolishly let Satan steal it away.

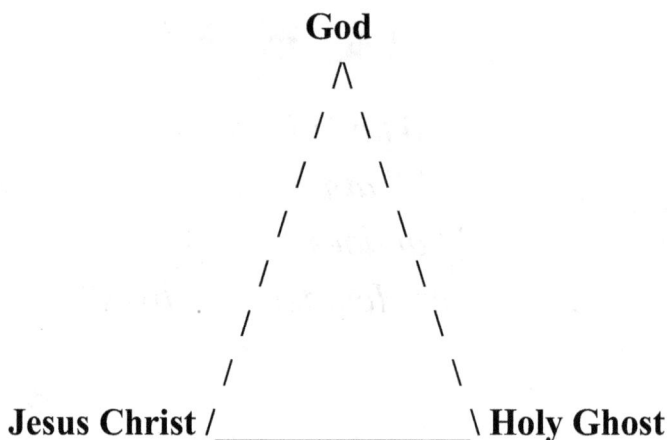

```
                    God
                    /\
                   /  \
                  /    \
                 /      \
                /        \
               /          \
              /            \
Jesus Christ /_____\ Holy Ghost
```

In addition to the numberless references to the different persons of the Godhead found throughout the word of God, there are certain passages which refer to all three members of the Trinity. Note the word Trinity is not found in the Bible, but we use it to denote the tri-unity of God.

You might say everybody knows that, but not everyone believes in the Trinity. Some believers are "two-list." They believe God is a person, that Jesus is a person, but the Holy Ghost is not a person; the Holy Ghost is the spirit or ghost of Jesus after He died on the cross. **Jesus isn't dead. He's alive and well.** I cannot personally believe this teaching. The Holy Ghost, as we shall see, has all the characteristics of being his own person.

Another belief is the "oneness" belief, which teaches that God, Jesus, and the Holy Ghost are not three, but all the same person. I don't doubt the salvation of the "two-list" or the "oneness" believers. I do have trouble with their doctrines. **If Jesus and God are the same person, then to whom did Jesus pray? Himself?** I hardly think so. **If Jesus, as scripture states, is seated at the right hand of God, then is Jesus seated at His own right hand?** Again, I think not. A "oneness" believer once said to me there aren't three Gods; there is only one God. I know I'm far from being smart. I, however, through the leading of the Holy Ghost, can see that **the Godhead is made up of three individual persons,** and all three work with one mind and in one accord; three in one and one in three.

The following scriptures prove a Divine Trinity of separate persons in the Godhead.

1. The word one means "one in unity as well as

one in number." It means unity in 1 John 5:7 as well as it does in John 17:11, 21-23.

1 John 5:7

> *For there are three that bear record in Heaven, the Father, the Word, and the Holy Ghost: and these three are one.*

John 17:11

> *And now I am no more in the world, but these are in the world, and I come to thee. Holy Father, keep through thine own name those whom thou hast given me, that they may be one; as we are.*

John 17:21-23

> *21 That they all may be one; as thou, Father, art in me, and I in thee, that they also may be one in us: that the world may believe that thou hast sent me.*
> *22 And the glory which thou gavest me I have given them; that they may be one, even as we are one.*
> *23 I in them, and thou in me, that they may*

be made perfect in one; and that the world may know that thou hast sent me, and hast loved them, as thou hast loved me.

Matthew 28:18-19

[18] And Jesus came and spake unto them, saying, All power is given unto me in heaven and in earth.
[19] Go ye therefore, and teach all nations, baptizing them in the name of the Father, and of the Son, and of the Holy Ghost:

Jesus is explaining the formula for water baptism. In this passage He's giving us a look at the Godhead. In His own words He tells us there are three. "The Father, the Son, and the Holy Ghost." **Water baptism does not wash away our sins and save us.** Salvation comes when we repent of our sins and ask Jesus to come into our life. While salvation comes when we accept Jesus as our Lord and Master, **water baptism is the outward sign to the world that there has been a change.** It symbolizes the death of the old man of sin as we go under the water, and the new man in Christ Jesus as we rise out of the water. The water doesn't save us; Jesus saves us by His blood washing us free from sin.

John 14:26

> *But the Comforter, which is the Holy Ghost, whom the Father will send in my name, he shall teach you all things, and bring all things to your remembrance, whatsoever I have said unto you.*

John 15:26

> *But when the Comforter is come, whom I will send unto you from the Father, even the Spirit of truth, which proceedeth from the Father, he shall testify of me:*

2. These three persons, the Father, the Word, and the Holy Ghost, are spoken of as one, each in number and individuality in scripture. There is one God the Father, one Lord Jesus Christ, and one Holy Ghost. These three make up the one triune Godhead.

1 Corinthians. 8:6

> *But to us there is but one God, the Father, of*

whom are all things, and we in Him; and one Lord Jesus Christ, by whom are all things, and we by Him.

Ephesians 4:3-6

[3] Endeavouring to keep the unity of the Spirit in the bond of peace.
[4] There is one body, and one Spirit, even as ye are called in one hope of your calling;
[5] One Lord, one faith, one baptism,
[6] One God and Father of all, who is above all, and though all, and in you all.

There are three separate persons in divine individuality and divine plurality: God the Father, God the Son, and God the Holy Ghost. Each is a separate individual with his own likes and dislikes, his own personality and feelings. Yet, together they make up one Godhead; a tri-une Godhead; and a divine plurality consisting of God the Father, God the Son, and God the Holy Ghost.

The Father is called God (1 Corinthians 8:6); the Son is called God (Isaiah 9:6-7, Hebrews 1:8, St. John 1:1-2 and 20:28); and the Holy Ghost is called God (Acts 5:3-4). As individual persons, each can be called God, and collectively they can be spoken of as God because of their perfect unity (Acts 2:32-33).

1 Corinthians 8:6

But to us there is but one God, the Father, of whom are all things, and we in him; and one Lord Jesus Christ, by whom are all things, and we by him.

Isaiah 9:6-7

[6] For unto us a child is born, unto us a son is given: and the government shall be upon his shoulder: and his name shall be called Wonderful, Counsellor, The mighty God, The everlasting Father, The Prince of Peace.

[7] Of the increase of his government and peace there shall be no end, upon the throne of David, and upon his kingdom, to order it, and to establish it with judgment and with justice from henceforth even for ever. The zeal of the LORD of hosts will perform this.

Hebrews 1:8

*But unto the Son he saith, Thy throne, O
God, is for ever and ever: a sceptre of righteousness is the sceptre of thy kingdom.*

John 1:1-2

*¹ In the beginning was the Word, and the
Word was with God, and the Word was God.
² The same was in the beginning with God.*

John 20:28

*And Thomas answered and said unto him,
My Lord and my God.*

Acts 5:3-4

*³ But Peter said, Ananias, why hath Satan
filled thine heart to lie to the Holy Ghost,
and to keep back part of the price of the
land?
⁴ Whiles it remained, was it not thine own?
and after it was sold, was it not in thine own
power? why hast thou conceived this thing
in thine heart? thou hast not lied unto men,*

but unto God.

Acts 2:32-33

> [32] *This Jesus hath God raised up, whereof we all are witnesses.*
> [33] *Therefore being by the right hand of God exalted, and having received of the Father the promise of the Holy Ghost, he hath shed forth this, which ye now see and hear.*

These scriptures reveal the truth of the tri-unity of the Godhead. A wealth of additional scriptures throughout the Bible further illustrate the triune nature of God. The last verse I leave with you on the Trinity or tri-unity of the Godhead is:

2 Corinthians 13:14

> *The grace of the Lord Jesus Christ, and the love of God, and the communion of the Holy Ghost, be with you all. Amen.*

Test Your Knowledge

1. What is the Godhead?

_____

_____

_____

2. How many are in the Godhead and who are they?

_____

_____

_____

_____

3. Who shall testify of Jesus?

_____

4. Can we lie to the Holy Ghost?

_____

5. How many bear record in Heaven and who are they?

_____

_____

6. What formula did Jesus give for water baptism?

_____

_____

_____

_____

_____

The Personality of the Holy Ghost

This membership of the Holy Ghost in the Holy Trinity is proof of the personality of the Holy Ghost. We too often think of the Holy Ghost as either the spirit of God or Jesus without His own personality. **We must begin to think of the Holy Ghost as a person.** He is not the spirit of God or Jesus. He has His own mind and feelings. Additional proof of the Holy Ghost's personality is found in his manifested attributes of personality. What does it take to be considered a person? What does the Word say that the Holy Ghost does in His work for God?

The following scripture tells of His work and His personality, character, and demeanor.

1. He strives with sinners.

Genesis 6:3

> *And the Lord said, My spirit shall not always strive with man, for that he also is flesh: yet his days shall be an hundred and twenty years.*

Here is a truth most people neglect; one many people don't even know. Ministers never teach it. The fact is: **God's spirit will not always strive with man.** Now's a good time to talk about God's spirit; God has a spirit just the same as we have. We sometimes think of the Holy Ghost as the spirit of God, but we're wrong, for the Holy Ghost is His own person with His own spirit. Because the Godhead is so unified in working together, it's very hard sometimes to see the difference between their personalities. Remember that the scripture teaches that the Holy Ghost would not come till Jesus went back to heaven. Before that time, the Holy Ghost worked in the background. After Jesus returned to sit at the right hand of God, then and only then did the Holy Ghost come to the forefront. Now, the Holy Ghost has come to be our comforter, to strive with sinners, and to bring conviction to the world. Genesis 6:3 tells us that man can—and sometimes does—sin away his days of grace. He reaches a place where God's spirit no longer deals with him. How long will God strive with a person? **Only God knows how long He will work with a person to get them to come to salvation.** There comes a time when God will turn them over to a reprobate mind.

Genesis 6:3

> *And the LORD said, My spirit shall not always strive with man, for that he also is flesh: yet his days shall be an hundred and twenty years.*

Romans 1:28

> *And even as they did not like to retain God in their knowledge, God gave them over to a reprobate mind, to do those things which are not convenient;*

2. He searches the heart.

Romans 8:27

> *And He that searcheth the hearts knoweth*

what is the mind of the Spirit, because he maketh intercession for the saints according to the will of God.

The Holy Ghost is the searcher of our hearts. What does He search for? He brings to our remembrance all things. Sometimes we may need to ask forgiveness for some idle thought or deed; or for hard feelings over an incident. We may face a need to draw closer to the Lord, or to lay aside some habit that hinders our spiritual growth. He knows what we need to improve our spiritual well-being. **He makes intercession before God on our behalf.**

3. He divides as He wills.

1 Corinthians 12:11

> *But all these worketh. that one and the self-same Spirit, dividing to every man severally as he will.*

Here we find the Holy Ghost dividing His spiritual gifts to the hearts of believers, as He (the Holy Ghost) sees fit. Let me be sure and add that

to receive the gifts of the Holy Ghost one must be baptized in the Holy Ghost with the evidence of speaking in other tongues. Thus, we see the Holy Ghost making the choices as to who will receive what gift. Note the Word does not say as God wishes, or as Christ wishes. The dividing of the gifts is left up to the giver of the gift, the precious Holy Ghost whose gifts are to be coveted. (This is one of the few times we are told to covet.)

1 Corinthians 12:31

> *But <u>covet earnestly</u> the best gifts: and yet shew I unto you a <u>more excellent</u> way. (*The underlining is the emphases of the author.)

4. He can be grieved.

Ephesians 4:30

> *And grieve not the Holy Spirit of God, whereby ye are sealed unto the day of redemption.*

"Grieve not." These words say a mouthful. **We are not to go back to those weak and** beggarly elements which condemn our souls and take away the love of God from our hearts. The scripture states:

Ephesians 4:17-18

> [17] *This I say therefore, and testify in the Lord, that ye henceforth walk not as other Gentiles walk, in the vanity of their mind.*
> [18] *Having the understanding darkened, being alienated from the life of God through the ignorance that is in them, because of the blindness of their heart:*

Therefore, let us lay aside those things, which hinder and grieve the Holy Ghost.

5. He can be vexed.

Isaiah 63:10

> *But they rebelled, and vexed His holy spirit: therefore He was turned to be their enemy, and He fought against them.*

To grieve is to do that which is not like unto

God; to vex is to repeatedly do that which you know the Lord is not pleased with; and thus the sweet and gentle Holy Ghost becomes vexed. The dictionary states: To grieve means to provoke to anger or displeasure by small irritations; annoy.

Thus we see that the Holy Ghost has a mind, a will, and emotions or feelings.

6. He teaches.

John 14:26

> *But the Comforter, which is the Holy Ghost, whom the Father will send in my name, he shall teach you all things, and bring all things to your remembrance, whatsoever I have said unto you.*

One of the main works of the Holy Ghost, as I see it, is teaching believers how to walk uprightly before God. **By placing conviction on the heart when we are about to do wrong or after we have made some sort of mistake, the Holy Ghost will instruct us and keep us on the right path.**

I have found as I read and study my Bible that the Holy Ghost will help me to understand

God's holy word. He teaches me how to seek the truth. He reveals to me those things that make me a better servant. He reveals hidden truths. Studying God's Word is like looking for gold. Some golden nuggets are found lying on the surface, but others have to be dug out. Dig deep and search out God's best; you will never be disappointed.

7. He testifies of Christ.

John 15:26

> *But when the Comforter is come, whom I will send unto you from the Father, even the Spirit of truth, which proceedeth from the Father, he shall testify of me:*

The Holy Ghost doesn't testify of himself, but He leads men and women to the Lord Jesus Christ. It is Jesus that saves the souls of lost mankind. **The Holy Ghost convicts man of his sins and draws them to the Savior.** He testifies of God's greatness. The Holy Ghost is a perfect gentleman, so He never goes where He isn't wanted. He is a very humble spirit, very gentle; and He is not boastful.

8. He reproves.

John 16:8

> *And when he is come, he will reprove the world of sin, and of righteousness, and of judgment:*

The Holy Ghost is now in the world. By His very presence the world is condemned, and sin is brought to light for what it really is, death to our soul. **He reproves us of sin so that we may walk with God.** The presence of the Holy Ghost brings to light those hidden sins. He reproves us and causes us to repent so that there is nothing that stands between us and God.

9. He guides.

John 16:13

> *Howbeit when he, the Spirit of truth, is come, he will guide you into all truth: for he shall not speak of Himself; but whatsoever he shall hear, that shall he speak: and he will shew you things to come.*

Romans 8:14

For as many as are led by the Spirit of God, they are the sons of God.

The work of the Holy Ghost, as we see here, is to lead us in the way of truth. **Those things He hears from God He delivers to the saints through tongues and interpretation, or by prophecy that the saints may become strong.** Let us never forget that the Holy Ghost may, and does, at sundry times, use the "Word of Wisdom" for the perfecting of the saints. This lets us know we are not alone, we are not forsaken, and the Lord is still in control of everything that has to do with His saints.

10. He comforts.

Acts 9:31

Then had the churches rest throughout all Judaea and Galilee and Samaria, and were edified; and walking in the fear of the Lord, and in the comfort of the Holy Ghost, were multiplied.

What a comfort to know that the Holy Ghost is with us and dwells within us, to comfort in all the curves that life holds. We know that in every problem Jesus is always with us and we are never alone. **The Holy Ghost is that special comforter that Jesus sends to lift us up when we are weak;** that special anointing that gives us peace in the midst of the storm; the ability to know that we know that we know we are saved, held in the arms of Jesus.

11. He helps our infirmities and intercedes for the saints.

Romans 8:26

> *Likewise the spirit also helpeth our infirmities: for we know not what we should pray for as we ought: but the Spirit itself maketh intercession for us with groanings which cannot be uttered.*

The work of the Holy Ghost is always in progress. As we look at the workings of the spirit, we need to remember that it is hard to separate each one, because they overlap. Here, we see that He helps our infirmities and intercedes for us.

Interceding for us is the same as helping our infirmities, though both are separate. The dictionary states that infirm is being feeble or weak or lacking firmness of purpose. Infirmity is a physical or mental defect. **Whatever the problem, spiritual or physical, the Holy Ghost goes before God in our behalf.** Just think for a moment how good it is to have the Holy Ghost go before God on our behalf, to intercede for us when we don't know what we need or how we should pray. The Holy Ghost knows what we need and asks God to give us the help and strength to overcome. To give us a comforter and intercessor to walk us through the difficult times, to stand beside us and speak God's love to us, reveals how much God cares about his people. **We can't fathom just how much Jesus and our Heavenly Father loves us, to send us this comforter, this precious Holy Ghost.** Thank God that we don't walk this way alone. We have a God who is in control, a Savior who redeems us from sin, and a Holy Ghost that inhabits us and takes care of us.

12. He searches the deep things of God.

1 Corinthians 2:10

But God hath revealed them unto us by his Spirit: for the Spirit searcheth all things, yea the deep things of God.

Many things in the word of God must be spiritually discerned. Discovering the truths in God's Word is like finding diamonds. Many precious gems lay on the surface to easily be picked up. Yet there are many that we must dig for, the deep things of God, wonderfully precious, but which can only be brought to light by the Holy Ghost. This is why we must study the word of God, so that as we study, the Holy Ghost can reveal to us the wonders of God and His word.

13. He sanctifies.

Romans 15:16

That I should be the minister of Jesus Christ to the Gentiles, ministering the gospel of God, that the offering up of the Gentiles might be acceptable, being sanctified by the Holy Ghost.

The most forgotten and most unpreached message of the Bible is the message of sanctification. Preachers are afraid to preach sanctification, because to do so you must get down to where people live out their everyday lives. **Sanctification concerns how we live, how we dress, the places we go, the things we do, and the words we use.** The Bible deals with all these things, and that's why people don't want to hear what "thus saith the Lord." It's all right to go to church and hear a sermon preached as long as it doesn't affect us or the things we want to do. But to serve God, the way God wants us to, we must conform to God's standards, which is exactly what people do not seem to want to do. We say we want to live for God, and we do, as long as it doesn't interfere with our own desires. **Sanctification is the putting away of anything that hinders our walk with God.** There is a biblical sanctification, which we all must adhere to, and then there is a personal sanctification, which is on a personal level between us and God.

14. He witnesses.

Romans 8:16

> *The Spirit itself beareth witness with our spirit, that we are the children of God:*

One of the greatest blessings that we can have is the witness of the spirit, whereby we can know that all is well between us and God. By this witness we can know that we are saved. We can know in whom we have believed, and we can build upon this assurance, with a "know-so" salvation, not a hope-so or a maybe-so salvation.

15. He commands.

Acts 16:6

> *Now when they had gone throughout Phrygia and the region of Galatia, and were forbidden of the Holy Ghost to preach the word in Asia.*

One very important work of the Holy Ghost is to speak to our hearts and tell us what He desires us to do, or what He would not have us to do. **If we will be obedient to his voice, we will avoid much of the trouble the devil tries to put upon us.** Obedience is better than sacrifice. Why should we sacrifice ourselves to Satan, when by obedience we can win the victory?

16. He is susceptible to personal treatment.

Acts 5:3

> *But Peter said, Ananias why hath Satan filled thine heart to lie to the Holy Ghost, and to keep back part of the price of the land?*

Surprise! Surprise! Did you know that you can lie to the Holy Ghost? Well, you can, not that you can get away with it, but you can lie to the Holy Ghost. Ananias and his wife thought they were lying to Peter, but they were wrong. We need to be careful lest we be found guilty of the same thing. **Always be truthful, for the truth will set you free.** The Lord knows the thoughts and the intents of our hearts, so why do we think we can get away with lying to the Holy Ghost or God?

17. He can be resisted.

Acts 7:51

> *Ye stiffnecked and uncircumcised in heart*

and ears, ye do always resist the Holy Ghost: as your fathers did, so do ye.

To resist the Holy Ghost is as simple as saying "no" when the Holy Ghost deals with your heart. Sinners resist the Holy Ghost when God's spirit deals with them to repent and they say "no," "not now," or "at a more convenient time." We resist the Holy Ghost when He tells us to go and pray for someone, and we won't go. We resist the Holy Ghost when He tells us to put a certain amount in the offering, and we reason that we can't afford it. When we are moved upon by God to do or say something and we refuse, then we resist the Holy Ghost.

18. He can be blasphemed.

Matthew 12:31-32

> [31] *Wherefore I say unto you, All manner of sin and blasphemy shall be forgiven unto men: but the blasphemy against the Holy Ghost shall not be forgiven unto men.*
> [32] *And whosoever speaketh a word against the Son of man, it shall be forgiven him: but*

whosoever speaketh against the Holy Ghost, it shall not be forgiven him, neither in this world, neither in the world to come.

What is blasphemy against the Holy Ghost? Finis Jennings Dake states: "It is any insulting remark or curse, even attributing to Satan the words of the Holy Ghost. It is unforgivable if it is done maliciously and knowingly."

Hebrews 6:4-9

[4] For it is impossible for those who were once enlightened, and have tasted of the heavenly gift, and were made partakers of the Holy Ghost,
[5] And have tasted the good word of God, and the powers of the world to come,
[6] If they shall fall away, to renew them again unto repentance; seeing they crucify to themselves the Son of God afresh, and put him to an open shame.
[7] For the earth which drinketh in the rain that cometh oft upon it, and bringeth forth

herbs meet for them by whom it is dressed, receiveth blessing from God:

⁸ But that which beareth thorns and briers is rejected, and is nigh unto cursing; whose end is to be burned.

⁹ But, beloved, we are persuaded better things of you, and things that accompany salvation, though we thus speak.

Blasphemy against the Holy Ghost, in my opinion and according to scripture, is this: After a person has been enlightened, has tasted of the heavenly gift, and has been made a partaker of the Holy Ghost, if they deny the reality of their experiences, they have committed blasphemy. These are people who know what it is to be saved and set free from sin, to be filled with the Holy Ghost and feel the very presence of God. **If, knowing all that has happened to them, they turn their backs on God and publicly deny all they have experienced, saying, "God is not real; the Holy Ghost baptism isn't real. It's all lies," is blasphemy against the Holy Ghost and will never be forgiven in this world, neither will it be forgiven in the world to come.**

19. He can be quenched.

1 Thessalonians 5:19

Quench not the Spirit.

To quench the spirit is to repress or suppress the emotional moving of the Holy Ghost.

Test Your Knowledge

1. What does the Word tell us to covet?

_____

2. Who is the Comforter?

_____

3. How does the Holy Ghost help our infirmi-ties?

_____

_____

_____

_____

_____

4. What is the blasphemy against the Holy Ghost?

_____

_____

_____

_____

_____

5. What will the Holy Ghost reprove the world of?

_____

_____

_____

_____

_____

6. What is sanctification, and why is it so important in the life of a Christian?

_____

_____

_____

_____

_____

The Difference Between Personality and Corporeity

There are those who have difficulty in distinguishing between personality (being a person) and corporeity (having a body). They cannot understand or believe that anything which is invisible and intangible, and which does not have a body, can be a person. The Word throughout the New Testament about the Holy Ghost refers to the Holy Ghost as "He" or "Him." In a few places, the Holy Ghost is referred to as the Holy Spirit, and in a few places as the spirit of God. But the Holy Ghost is not the spirit of God. **The Holy Ghost is a person in His own right.** He is the third person in the triune Godhead. There is a dangerous trend in the Pentecostal movement to refer to the Holy Ghost as the Holy Spirit and, even more so, as the spirit of God. When we refer to the Holy Ghost as the Holy Spirit or the spirit of God, we are taking away the person-ship of the Holy Ghost. This should not be done. The Holy Ghost is a person in His own right.

Luke 24:39

> *Behold my hands and my feet, that it is I my-self: handle me, and see; for a spirit hath not flesh and bones, as ye see me have.*

John 4:24

> *God is a Spirit: and they that worship him must worship him in spirit and in truth.*

John 1:18

> *No man hath seen God at any time; the only begotten Son, which is in the bosom of the Father, He hath declared Him.*

We must believe that the Holy Ghost is a person in the sense that He has all the emotions we have, yet He is not confined to a body such as we are. God is a spirit, thus He is everywhere at the same time. Jesus, when He was on the earth and in his earthly body, was confined in one place at any given time. The Holy Ghost, to perform the Father's will, must be a spirit. **The Holy Ghost ministry is worldwide, so He cannot be confined to a body. But, most certainly, He is a person.** The work of the Holy Ghost is partly stated in St. John 16:7-15.

John 16:7-15

⁷ Nevertheless I tell you the truth; It is expedient for you that I go away: for if I go not away, the Comforter will not come unto you; but if I depart, I will send him unto you.
⁸ And when He is come, he will reprove the world of sin, and of righteousness, and of judgment:
⁹ Of sin, because they believe not on me;
¹⁰ Of righteousness, because I go to my Father, and ye see me no more;
¹¹ Of judgment, because the prince of this world is judged.
¹² I have yet many things to say unto you, but ye can not bear them now.
¹³ Howbeit when he, the Spirit of truth, is come, he will guide you into all truth: for he

shall not speak of himself; but whatsoever he shall hear, that shall He speak: and he will shew you things to come.

14 He shall glorify me: for he shall receive of mine, and shall shew it unto you.

15 All things that the Father hath are mine: therefore said I, that he shall take of mine, and shall shew it unto you.

The Holy Ghost in Conversion

The Holy Ghost plays a very important part in the conversion of sinners, for it is the work of the Holy Ghost to convict us of sin.

John 16:8

> *When he is come, he will reprove the world of sin, and of righteousness, and of judgment.*

The Holy Ghost brings conviction to our hearts and makes us realize we have sinned and are lost and on a downward road to a devil's hell without God. The general theme of the church today is to preach a social gospel. There's no room for hellfire and brimstone messages in today's church. Such preaching scares people, upsets their lives, and undermines their sense of security. I sincerely hope this is the case, for **the last thing we need is a sense of false security.**

We read in the Word that the fear of the Lord is the beginning of wisdom. It does us very little good to preach a gospel that's only part of the truth. The love of God is a great message, but at the same time the full gospel tells us that, yes, there's a heaven to gain, but at the same time there's a very real hell we must shun. The Word tells us we cannot do our own thing, but we must walk in the holiness of God. Without holiness, no man shall see God. **Ministers who refuse to preach the full truth of the gospel are keeping the Holy Ghost from performing his work.** Without the full gospel message, the Holy Ghost has His hands tied and cannot bring conviction to a heart that has not been warned of sin. These ministers are condemning their people to eternity without God. They become blind leaders of the blind, and they will both fall into the ditch together.

People want a gospel that's easy to live, without trials and temptations. But the Word tells us we will be tried as by fire. **Teaching that the child of God doesn't suffer trials and temptation is an outright lie of the devil.** If we can be fooled into believing there's no hell, then we have no fear of God and are not compelled to give ourselves totally unto God. **The Holy Ghost places conviction in our hearts—fear if you please, for it's a fearful thing to fall into the hands of a living God.** The Holy Ghost conviction is what causes us to cry out to God. That fear, after we give our hearts to Jesus, turns into a love so sweet that words cannot fully explain it.

Proverbs 9:10

> *The fear of the Lord is the beginning of wisdom: and the knowledge of the holy is understanding.*

1 Corinthians 12:3

> *Wherefore I give you to understand, that no man speaking by the spirit of God calleth Jesus accursed: and that no man can say that Jesus is the Lord, but by the Holy Ghost.*

This doesn't mean that everyone who says "Jesus is Lord" is saved. It means that those who have a real change of heart, through Holy Ghost conviction of sin, can call Jesus "Lord." For only then can they truly realize what it means for Jesus to be "Lord." We must be born again; the blood must wash away our sins.

2 Thessalonians 2:13

> *But we are bound to give thanks always to God for you, brethren beloved of the Lord, because God hath from the beginning chosen you to salvation through sanctification of the Spirit and belief of the truth.*

Again, we come to the word sanctification. A quick definition is: "It is the separation of ourselves from sin, the laying aside or laying down of those things which entangle us in the world." Sanctification works in two ways. There's a biblical sanctification we must all come under. It's the same for everybody, with no exceptions. **Then there's a personal sanctification, where God tests your obedience to his will.** You may be asked to do something or give up something that no one else is asked to do, just to see if you will be obedient to His will in your life.

1 Peter 2:1, 2

[1] Wherefore laying aside all malice, and all guile, and hypocrisies, and envies, and all evil speaking.
[2] As newborn babes, desire the sincere milk of the word, that ye may grow thereby.

1 Peter 1:2

Elect according to the foreknowledge of God the Father, through sanctification of the spirit, unto obedience and sprinkling of the blood of Jesus Christ: Grace unto you and peace be multiplied.

The Holy Ghost Baptism

When we are saved, we receive the spirit of Christ. This means Jesus comes into our hearts to dwell. We are changed from the old man of sin into a new creature. Our sins are washed away, or more properly, our sins are covered by the shed blood of Jesus Christ. This process of salvation is only one of the works of the Holy Ghost. It is the Holy Ghost that draws us to God, that brings conviction to our hearts and souls and shows us how lost a state we are in. The Word teaches us that no man cometh unto the Father except the spirit draws him. **The baptism of the Holy Ghost is a completely different experience from salvation.** Holy Ghost baptism comes when we invite, through prayer, the Holy Ghost to come into our lives and hearts.

Before the Holy Ghost will come into our hearts, we must first prepare ourselves to receive Him. Only when our hearts are sanctified before

God will the Holy Ghost come in to dwell. What does it take to receive the Holy Ghost? **Sometimes, not being completely surrendered to the Lord will keep a person from receiving the baptism.** In the case of one person who sought the baptism for twenty years, she would get close, laugh in the spirit, lay on the floor lost in the spirit for hours, but would never go through to the baptism of the Holy Ghost with the evidence of speaking in other tongues. When the night finally came that she received the baptism, she stated afterward that all along, the only thing that stood in the way was her fear of what she would do after she received the Holy Ghost. She was a very shy, timid person, and she was afraid that she might do some of the things that she had seen others do, such as dance in the spirit, roll on the floor, run the isles or whatever. This was enough to keep her from receiving the Holy Ghost, even though she sought it for twenty years. **The one thing that we must remember is that the Holy Ghost is a perfect gentleman and will never go against our will.**

To receive, we must completely and totally surrender. We must give ourselves over to the Holy Ghost and let Him have complete control in whatever He wants to say and/or do. It goes against our nature to give up control of our bodies, but we must to receive. Then and only then will we receive the Holy Ghost into our hearts. The most important principal a child of God must learn is this, that to have a relationship with God we must learn to totally surrender our lives and will into His hands. **If there is to be a unity between God and man, we must learn to put our trust in God and leave it there regardless of the circumstances of life.**

Symbols of the Holy Ghost

Four principal symbols for the Holy Ghost appear in the Bible as seen in the following passages:

Oil:

Matthew 25:4, 8

> *⁴ But the wise took oil in their vessels with their lamps.*
> *⁸ And the foolish said unto the wise, 'Give us of your oil; for our lamps are gone out.'*

Here we see that the ten were virgins, meaning they were church members or believers. The "oil" denotes the Holy Ghost. While the bridegroom tarried, all slumbered and slept; then the cry went out to prepare to meet the bridegroom. When they "arose"—indicating the rapture—we find half of the church was backslidden.

The oil stands for the Holy Ghost just as the virgins are a symbol for salvation. **We can't be misled, thinking the oil represents God's spirit.** You don't have to have the Holy Ghost to go to heaven. In this passage, when a person begins to backslide, the Holy Ghost (the oil in the virgins' lamps) leaves first. Then, because of sin, they turn their back on God. **A believer can lose the Holy Ghost but keep their salvation.** That which is used, develops, while that which is not used, wastes away. One of our greatest concerns should be not allowing ourselves to spiritually "go to sleep." For the Son of Man cometh in an hour that you think not, therefore watch and pray so that day takes you not unaware.

As the oil represents the Holy Ghost, it also represents the anointing, for as oil was used to anoint kings, it was also used to anoint vessels to the service of the Lord. **To be filled with the Holy Ghost is to be "anointed" into God's service.** In the Old Testament, the anointing represents a divine dedication and a consecration to a holy office. After we have received the Holy Ghost, we have been anointed by God to be preachers, teachers and intercessors before God for the lost and the dying.

Wind:

John 3:8

> *The wind bloweth where it listeth, and thou hearest the sound thereof, but canst not tell whence it cometh, and whither it goeth: so is every one that is born of the Spirit.*

Acts 2:2

> *And suddenly there came a sound from heaven as of a rushing mighty wind, and it filled all the house where they were sitting.*

The wind denotes the coming presence of the Holy Ghost such as in the book of Acts. If we look at man in creation we see that after man was formed God breathed into Adam the breath of life. Or blow into man the breath of life. Jesus also breathed upon his disciples and said "Receive ye the Holy Ghost" (John 20:22). Can we say that he blew upon them his very breath the breath of life?

Water:

John 7:37-39

> *37 In the last day, that great day of the feast, Jesus stood and cried, saying, If any man thirst, let him come to me, and drink.*
> *38 He that believeth on me as the scripture hath said, out of his belly shall flow rivers of living water.*
> *39 (But this spake he of the Spirit, which they that believe on him should receive: for the Holy Ghost was not yet given; because that Jesus was not yet glorified.)*

To the woman at the well, Jesus spoke of a water whereof she would never thirst again, that it would become a well of water springing up unto everlasting life. Water is essential to all living things. Without water nothing can live. In the spirit it is the same, for **without the divine presence of our Savior, God's Holy Son, there is no life.**

Dove:

John 1:32

And John bare record, saying, I saw the Spirit descending from heaven like a dove, and it abode upon him.

Tender, gentle, pure and harmless like a dove, the Holy Ghost is easily frightened or grieved. And, as the dove is a universal symbol of peace, so **the Holy Ghost is God's agent to bring peace to the human heart.**

The Importance of the Holy Ghost

The scripture states the following:

Luke 24:49

> *And, behold, I send the promise of my Father upon you: but tarry ye in the city of Jerusalem until ye be endued with power from on high.*

Acts 1:8

> *But ye shall receive power after that the Holy Ghost is come upon you: and ye shall be witnesses unto me both in Jerusalem, and in all Judaea , and in Samaria, and unto the uttermost part of the earth.*

The importance can be listed as follows:

1. God provided the Holy Ghost for us.

John 14:16

> *And I will pray the Father, and he shall give you another Comforter, that he may abide with you for ever;*

2. Jesus received the Holy Ghost.

Matthew 3:16

> *And Jesus, when he was baptized, went up straightway out of the water: and, lo, the heavens were opened unto him, and he saw the Spirit of God descending like a dove, and lighting upon him:*

3. Jesus commanded his disciples to go and tarry for the Holy Ghost.

Luke 24:49

> *And, behold, I send the promise of my*

Father upon you: but tarry ye in the city of Jerusalem, until ye be endued with power from on high.

4. All his disciples received the Holy Ghost as well as the rest of the 120.

Acts 2:4

And they were all filled with the Holy Ghost, and began to speak with other tongues, as the Spirit gave them utterance.

5. The Holy Ghost affected the conversion of 3,000 on the day of Pentecost.

Acts 2:37-41

37 Now when they heard this, they were pricked in their heart, and said unto Peter and to the rest of the apostles, Men and brethren, what shall we do?
38 Then Peter said unto them, Repent, and be baptized every one of you in the name of Jesus Christ for the remission of sins, and ye

shall receive the gift of the Holy Ghost.

[39] For the promise is unto you, and to your children, and to all that are afar off, even as many as the Lord our God shall call.

[40] And with many other words did he testify and exhort, saying, Save yourselves from this untoward generation.

[41] Then they that gladly received his word were baptized: and the same day there were added unto them about three thousand souls.

6. The Holy Ghost enabled the apostles to fill Jerusalem with the doctrine of Christ.

Acts 2:14

But Peter, standing up with the eleven, lifted up his voice, and said unto them, Ye men of Judaea, and all ye that dwell at Jerusalem, be this known unto you, and hearken to my words:

Acts 4:31

And when they had prayed, the place was

shaken where they were assembled together; and they were all filled with the Holy Ghost, and they spake the word of God with boldness.

7. The Holy Ghost enabled the 120 to perform supernatural signs and wonders.

Acts 2:43

And fear came upon every soul: and many wonders and signs were done by the apostles.

8. The Holy Ghost enabled the saints to spread the gospel to the rest of the world.

Acts 1:8

But ye shall receive power, after that the Holy Ghost is come upon you: and ye shall be witnesses unto me both in Jerusalem, and in all Judaea, and in Samaria, and unto the uttermost part of the earth.

9. The saints were careful to lead their converts into the same experience.
Acts 2:38-41

38 Then Peter said unto them, Repent, and be baptized every one of you in the name of Jesus Christ for the remission of sins, and ye shall receive the gift of the Holy Ghost.
39 For the promise is unto you, and to your children, and to all that are afar off, even as many as the Lord our God shall call.
40 And with many other words did he testify and exhort, saying, Save yourselves from this untoward generation.
41 Then they that gladly received his word were baptized: and the same day there were added unto them about three thousand souls.

10. Christ commanded all believers to be filled with the Holy Ghost.

Acts 1:4-5

4 And, being assembled together with them, commanded them that they should not de-

part from Jerusalem, but wait for the prom-
ise of the Father, which, saith he, ye have
heard of me.
⁵ For John truly baptized with water; but ye
shall be baptized with the Holy Ghost not
many days hence.

As we look at this list, we can see a great responsibility to spread the word of God, to fulfill our duty to see as many saved and filled with the Holy Ghost as quickly as possible before it's too late.

Test Your Knowledge

1. What is the difference between personality and corporeity?

_____

_____

_____

_____

2. What does the Holy Ghost do in the conversion of sinners?

_____

_____

_____

_____

3. What is the baptism of the Holy Ghost, and how does it differ from salvation?

_____

_____

_____

_____

_____

4. Name the symbols of the Holy Ghost.

_____

_____

_____

_____

_____

5. List four important things that the Holy Ghost does.

_____

_____

_____

_____

_____

The Initial Physical Evidence

The initial evidence that a person has received the Holy Ghost is that they speak in other tongues as the spirit gives them utterance.

Acts 2:4

> *And they were all filled with the Holy Ghost, and began to speak with other tongues as the Spirit gave them utterance.*

1 Corinthians 14:22

> *Wherefore tongues are for a sign, not to them that believe, but to them that believe not: but prophesying serveth not for them that believe not, but for them which believe.*

The sign of the Holy Ghost baptism is speaking in other tongues as the spirit gives utterance. Contrary to what a major part of the Christian world says and teaches, **you cannot have the Holy Ghost without the initial sign or evidence.** Just as you cannot have salvation without a drastic change in your lifestyle, you cannot have the Holy Ghost without the tongues. **Tongues come from the Holy Ghost Himself;** He gives you the tongues He wants you to have. Preachers and churches that try to teach people how to speak in tongues and hold classes to teach tongues are strictly of the devil. I don't care how big the preacher, the church, or the denomination, if the Holy Ghost doesn't give it to you, it's not worth having. Anything else is false.

Tongues in the Church

Tongues serve a very important service in the church. God uses tongues in two completely different ways. *ONE*: The church knows when someone has received the Holy Ghost baptism. **Tongues is the initial sign or evidence that one has received the Holy Ghost.** This is God's way of saying to the world that this one has received the promise of the Father. *TWO*: **Tongues and interpretation equal prophecy.** The Lord moves upon an individual to deliver a message in tongues to the congregation. Then the Lord moves upon another person to interpret the message that was delivered in tongues. Sometimes the person who delivered the message will interpret the message, if no one else will yield to the spirit. At times, no one will interpret the message. The message can be to one person or to the whole congregation. The message can be about the future, our condition with God, words of encouragement, or whatever the

Lord wants us to know. To get a well-rounded look at tongues, we need to study the whole of 1 Corinthians, Chapter 14.

1 Corinthians 14:1-40

> *[1] Follow after charity, and desire spiritual gifts, but rather that ye may prophesy.*
> *[2] For he that speaketh in an unknown tongue speaketh not unto men, but unto God: for no man understandeth him; howbeit in the spirit he speaketh mysteries.*
> *[3] But he that prophesieth speaketh unto men to edification, and exhortation, and comfort.*
> *[4] He that speaketh in an unknown tongue edifieth himself; but he that prophesieth edifieth the church.*
> *[5] I would that ye all spake with tongues, but rather that ye prophesied: for greater is he that prophesieth than he that speaketh with tongues, except he interpret, that the church may receive edifying.*
> *[6] Now, brethren, if I come unto you speaking with tongues, what shall I profit you, except I shall speak to you either by revelation, or by knowledge, or by prophesying, or by doctrine?*

⁷ And even things without life giving sound, whether pipe or harp, except they give a distinction in the sounds, how shall it be known what is piped or harped?

⁸ For if the trumpet give an uncertain sound, who shall prepare himself to the battle?

⁹ So likewise ye, except ye utter by the tongue words easy to be understood, how shall it be known what is spoken? for ye shall speak into the air.

¹⁰ There are, it may be, so many kinds of voices in the world, and none of them is without signification.

¹¹ Therefore if I know not the meaning of the voice, I shall be unto him that speaketh a barbarian, and he that speaketh shall be a barbarian unto me. ¹² Even so ye, forasmuch as ye are zealous of spiritual gifts, seek that ye may excel to the edifying of the church.

¹³ Wherefore let him that speaketh in an unknown tongue pray that he may interpret.

¹⁴ For if I pray in an unknown tongue, my spirit prayeth, but my understanding is unfruitful.

¹⁵ What is it then? I will pray with the spirit, and I will pray with the understanding also:

I will sing with the spirit, and I will sing with the understanding also.

16 Else when thou shalt bless with the spirit, how shall he that occupieth the room of the unlearned say Amen at thy giving of thanks, seeing he understandeth not what thou sayest?

17 For thou verily givest thanks well, but the other is not edified.

18 I thank my God, I speak with tongues more than ye all:

19 Yet in the church I had rather speak five words with my understanding, that by my voice I might teach others also, than ten thousand words in an unknown tongue.

20 Brethren, be not children in understanding: howbeit in malice be ye children, but in understanding be men.

21 In the law it is written, With men of other tongues and other lips will I speak unto this people; and yet for all that will they not hear me, saith the Lord.

22 Wherefore tongues are for a sign, not to them that believe, but to them that believe not: but prophesying serveth not for them that believe not, but for them which believe.

23 If therefore the whole church be come to-

gether into one place, and all speak with tongues, and there come in those that are unlearned, or unbelievers, will they not say that ye are mad?

24 But if all prophesy, and there come in one that believeth not, or one unlearned, he is convinced of all, he is judged of all:

25 And thus are the secrets of his heart made manifest; and so falling down on his face he will worship God, and report that God is in you of a truth.

26 How is it then, brethren? when ye come together, every one of you hath a psalm, hath a doctrine, hath a tongue, hath a reve-lation, hath an interpretation. Let all things be done unto edifying.

27 If any man speak in an unknown tongue, let it be by two, or at the most by three, and that by course; and let one interpret.

28 But if there be no interpreter, let him keep silence in the church; and let him speak to himself, and to God.

29 Let the prophets speak two or three, and let the other judge.

30 If any thing be revealed to another that sitteth by, let the first hold his peace.

31 For ye may all prophesy one by one, that

all may learn, and all may be comforted.

32 And the spirits of the prophets are subject to the prophets.

33 For God is not the author of confusion, but of peace, as in all churches of the saints.

34 Let your women keep silence in the churches: for it is not permitted unto them to speak; but they are commanded to be under obedience, as also saith the law.

35 And if they will learn any thing, let them ask their husbands at home: for it is a shame for women to speak in the church.

36 What? came the word of God out from you? or came it unto you only?

37 If any man think himself to be a prophet, or spiritual, let him acknowledge that the things that I write unto you are the commandments of the Lord. 38 But if any man be ignorant, let him be ignorant.

39 Wherefore, brethren, covet to prophesy, and forbid not to speak with tongues.

40 Let all things be done decently and in order.

Spiritual Gifts

It's a sad fact that in today's world, the church is sadly ignorant of the spiritual workings of God. In most churches the gifts of the Holy Ghost are cast aside because they do not fit into their program. They have no place in the worship service, because God and the moving of the Spirit are foreign to the church world. This condition is almost as bad in the Pentecostal churches of today. **If you ask how many gifts of the spirit there are, most people cannot tell you, much less name them.** There are nine main gifts with many subdivisions, but we will focus on the nine major ones. We will also break them down into three classifications.

1 Corinthians 12:1-31

[1] Now concerning spiritual gifts, brethren, I

would not have you ignorant.

² Ye know that ye were Gentiles, carried away unto these dumb idols, even as ye were led.

³ Wherefore I give you to understand, that no man speaking by the Spirit of God calleth Jesus accursed: and that no man can say that Jesus is the Lord, but by the Holy Ghost.

⁴ Now there are diversities of gifts, but the same Spirit.

⁵ And there are differences of administrations, but the same Lord.

⁶ And there are diversities of operations, but it is the same God which worketh all in all.

⁷ But the manifestation of the Spirit is given to every man to profit withal. ⁸ For to one is given by the Spirit the word of wisdom; to another the word of knowledge by the same Spirit;

⁹ To another faith by the same Spirit; to another the gifts of healing by the same Spirit;

¹⁰ To another the working of miracles; to another prophecy; to another discerning of spirits; to another divers kinds of tongues; to another the interpretation of tongues:

¹¹ But all these worketh that one and the

selfsame Spirit, dividing to every man sever-
ally as he will.

¹² For as the body is one, and hath many
members, and all the members of that one
body, being many, are one body: so also is
Christ.

¹³ For by one Spirit are we all baptized into
one body, whether we be Jews or Gentiles,
whether we be bond or free; and have been
all made to drink into one Spirit.

¹⁴ For the body is not one member, but
many.

¹⁵ If the foot shall say, Because I am not the
hand, I am not of the body; is it therefore
not of the body?

¹⁶ And if the ear shall say, Because I am not
the eye, I am not of the body; is it therefore
not of the body?

¹⁷ If the whole body were an eye, where were
the hearing? If the whole were hearing,
where were the smelling?

¹⁸ But now hath God set the members every
one of them in the body, as it hath pleased
him.

¹⁹ And if they were all one member, where
were the body?

²⁰ But now are they many members, yet but

one body.

²¹ And the eye cannot say unto the hand, I have no need of thee: nor again the head to the feet, I have no need of you.

²² Nay, much more those members of the body, which seem to be more feeble, are necessary:

²³ And those members of the body, which we think to be less honourable, upon these we bestow more abundant honour; and our uncomely parts have more abundant comeliness.

²⁴ For our comely parts have no need: but God hath tempered the body together, having given more abundant honour to that part which lacked: ²⁵ That there should be no schism in the body; but that the members should have the same care one for another.

²⁶ And whether one member suffer, all the members suffer with it; or one member be honoured, all the members rejoice with it.

²⁷ Now ye are the body of Christ, and members in particular.

²⁸ And God hath set some in the church, first apostles, secondarily prophets, thirdly teachers, after that miracles, then gifts of healings, helps, governments, diversities of

tongues.

²⁹ Are all apostles? are all prophets? are all teachers? are all workers of miracles?

³⁰ Have all the gifts of healing? do all speak with tongues? do all interpret? ³¹ But covet earnestly the best gifts: and yet shew I unto you a more excellent way.

Gifts Classified

1. There are three gifts of *Revelation*
    1. The gift of Wisdom
    2. The gift of Knowledge
    3. The gift of Discerning of Spirits
2. There are three gifts of *Power*
    1. The gift of Faith
    2. The gift of Miracles
    3. The gift of Healing
3. There are three gifts of *Utterance*
    1. The gift of Prophecy
    2. The gift of Tongues
    3. The gift of Interpretation

The Greatest Gift in Each Class

In the gifts of **Revelation** . . . the greatest gift is the word of . . .

— *Wisdom* —

In the gifts of **Power** . . . the greatest gift is the gift of . . .

— *Faith* —

In the gifts of **Utterance** . . . the greatest gift is the gift of . . .

— *Prophecy* —

Wisdom

Wisdom is the greatest gift in its class, because wisdom is the ability to use our knowledge wisely. **Knowledge is knowing about different subjects, the ins and outs, how they work. Wisdom uses that knowledge to its greatest fulfillment.** The discerning of spirits is the process of letting the Lord spiritually reveal to our spirit the conditions around us. Wisdom and the leading of the Lord then tell us how to handle the problems that lie before us. No wonder the scripture tells us to seek for wisdom.

Faith

Faith is the greatest gift in its class, for without faith none of the other gifts could operate. The gift of healing refers to divine power, to effect deliverance from sickness and disease. The gift of miracles is the gift where there exists the creative element.

Matthew 17:20

> *And Jesus said unto them, Because of your unbelief: for verily I say unto you, If ye have faith as a grain of mustard seed, ye shall say unto this mountain, Remove hence to yonder place; and it shall remove; and nothing shall be impossible unto you."*

Prophecy

Prophecy is the greatest gift in its class. Tongues are divine utterances, straight from God's throne room. Interpretation of tongues is, through the spirit, the message given to some willing and yielded person to deliver so all may hear from God.

1 Corinthians 13:1-11

> *¹ Though I speak with the tongues of men and of angels, and have not charity, I am become as sounding brass, or a tinkling cymbal.*
> *² And though I have the gift of prophecy, and understand all mysteries, and all knowledge; and though I have all faith, so that I could remove mountains, and have not charity, I am nothing.*
> *³ And though I bestow all my goods to feed*

the poor, and though I give my body to be burned, and have not charity, it profiteth me nothing.

4 Charity suffereth long, and is kind; charity envieth not; charity vaunteth not itself, is not puffed up,

5 Doth not behave itself unseemly, seeketh not her own, is not easily provoked, thinketh no evil;

6 Rejoiceth not in iniquity, but rejoiceth in the truth;

7 Beareth all things, believeth all things, hopeth all things, endureth all things.

8 Charity never faileth: but whether there be prophecies, they shall fail; whether there be tongues, they shall cease; whether there be knowledge, it shall vanish away.

9 For we know in part, and we prophesy in part.

10 But when that which is perfect is come, then that which is in part shall be done away.

11 When I was a child, I spake as a child, I understood as a child, I thought as a child: but when I became a man, I put away childish things.

1 Corinthians 12:27-31

²⁷ *Now ye are the body of Christ, and members in particular.*

²⁸ *And God hath set some in the church, first apostles, secondarily prophets, thirdly, teachers, after that miracles, then gifts of healings, helps, governments, diversities of tongues.*

²⁹ *Are all apostles? are all prophets? are all teachers? are all workers of miracles?*

³⁰ *Have all the gifts of healing? do all speak with tongues? do all interpret?*

³¹ *But covet earnestly the best gifts: and yet shew I unto you a more excellent way.*

The Nine Spiritual Gifts

Knowledge

Knowledge is knowing. We gain knowledge in many ways in the natural. We learn skills by doing and by reading. **Before you can teach someone, you must first know about the subject.** It's hard to teach a subject you don't know firsthand. So we see that knowledge is "knowing." **The gift of the Word of Knowledge is simply knowledge that is given to us by God concerning the scriptures and spiritual interpretation,** on those subjects in which God would have us to be well-versed, so that by using this gift, we can be a help to those who are around us. This imparting of knowledge to others makes their lives easier.

Genesis 3:5-6, 22-23

5 For God doth know that in the day ye eat

thereof, then your eyes shall be opened, and ye shall be as gods, knowing good and evil.

⁶ And when the woman saw that the tree was good for food, and that it was pleasant to the eyes, and a tree to be desired to make one wise, she took of the fruit thereof, and did eat, and gave also unto her husband with her; and he did eat.

²² And the Lord God said, Behold, the man is become as one of us, to know good and evil: and now, lest he put forth his hand, and take also of the tree of life, and eat, and live for ever:

²³ Therefore the Lord God sent him forth from the garden of Eden, to till the ground from whence he was taken.

1 Corinthians 8:1-2

¹ Now as touching things offered unto idols, we know that we all have knowledge. Knowledge puffeth up, but charity edifieth.

² And if any man think that he knoweth any thing, he knoweth nothing yet as he ought to know.

Proverbs 2:3-5

3 Yea, if thou criest after knowledge, and liftest up thy voice for understanding;
4 If thou seekest her as silver, and searchest for her as for hid treasures;
5 Then shalt thou understand the fear of the Lord, and find the knowledge of God.

Proverbs 15:19

The way of the slothful man is as an hedge of thorns: but the way of the righteous is made plain.

James 3:13

Who is a wise man and endued with knowledge among you? let him shew out of a good conversation his works with meekness of wisdom.

Wisdom

Wisdom builds with the materials which knowledge provides. Wisdom understands facts, laws, principles, trends, influences, possibilities and inevitabilities. The Bible says, "The fear of the Lord is the beginning of wisdom." **Knowledge is fruitless if we do not possess the ability to use what we have learned.** We express wisdom in our lives daily by the decisions we make, after judging all of our alternatives. We have often heard it said that a person has no common sense. What this simply means is that he cannot put his knowledge to work. Book learning and practical application are two entirely different things. Wisdom is the ability to use your knowledge correctly.

Isaiah 11:2

And the spirit of the Lord shall rest upon

him, the spirit of wisdom and understanding, the spirit of counsel and might, the spirit of knowledge and of the fear of the Lord;

Proverbs 4:5-13

⁵ Get wisdom, get understanding: forget it not; neither decline from the words of my mouth.
⁶ Forsake her not, and she shall preserve thee: love her, and she shall keep thee.
⁷ Wisdom is the principal thing; therefore get wisdom: and with all thy getting get understanding.
⁸ Exalt her, and she shall promote thee: she shall bring thee to honour, when thou dost embrace her.
⁹ She shall give to thine head an ornament of grace: a crown of glory shall she deliver to thee.
¹⁰ Hear, O my son, and receive my sayings; and the years of thy life shall be many.
¹¹ I have taught thee in the way of wisdom; I have led thee in right paths.
¹² When thou goest, thy steps shall not be straitened; and when thou runnest, thou shalt not stumble.

13 Take fast hold of instruction; let her not go: keep her; for she is thy life.

James 1:5-8

5 If any of you lack wisdom, let him ask of God, that giveth to all men liberally, and upbraideth not; and it shall be given him.
6 But let him ask in faith, nothing wavering. For he that wavereth is like a wave of the sea driven with the wind and tossed.
7 For let not that man think that he shall re-ceive any thing of the Lord.
8 A double minded man is unstable in all his ways.

James 3:13-18

13 Who is a wise man and endued with knowledge among you? let him shew out of a good conversation his works with meek-ness of wisdom.
14 But if ye have bitter envying and strife in your hearts, glory not, and lie not against the truth.
15 This wisdom descendeth not from above, but is earthly, sensual, devilish.

16 For where envying and strife is, there is confusion and every evil work.

17 But the wisdom that is from above is first pure, then peaceable, gentle, and easy to be intreated, full of mercy and good fruits, without partiality, and without hypocrisy.

18 And the fruit of righteousness is sown in peace of them that make peace.

Proverbs 9:10

The fear of the Lord is the beginning of wisdom: and the knowledge of the holy is understanding.

James 3:17

But the wisdom that is from above is first pure, then peaceable, gentle, and easy to be intreated, full of mercy and good fruits, without partiality, and without hypocrisy.

Discerning of Spirits

Discerning of Spirits is such an important phase of spiritual knowledge, that it is honored with recognition apart from the gift of the Word of Knowledge. The reason for this lies in the value which this gift has in Christian life and ministry.

1 Kings 3:9

> *Give therefore thy servant an understanding heart to judge thy people, that I may discern between good and bad: for who is able to judge this thy so great a people?*

1 Corinthians 2:9-16

> *[9] But as it is written, Eye hath not seen, nor ear heard, neither have entered into the*

heart of man, the things which God hath prepared for them that love him.

10 But God hath revealed them unto us by his Spirit: for the Spirit searcheth all things, yea, the deep things of God.

11 For what man knoweth the things of a man, save the spirit of man which is in him? even so the things of God knoweth no man, but the Spirit of God.

12 Now we have received, not the spirit of the world, but the spirit which is of God; that we might know the things that are freely given to us of God.

13 Which things also we speak, not in the words which man's wisdom teacheth, but which the Holy Ghost teacheth; comparing spiritual things with spiritual.

14 But the natural man receiveth not the things of the Spirit of God: for they are foolishness unto him: neither can he know them, because they are spiritually discerned.

15 But he that is spiritual judgeth all things, yet he himself is judged of no man.

16 For who hath known the mind of the Lord, that he may instruct him? But we have the mind of Christ.

Hebrews 5:12-14

12 For when for the time ye ought to be teachers, ye have need that one teach you again which be the first principles of the oracles of God; and are become such as have need of milk, and not of strong meat.

13 For every one that useth milk is unskilful in the word of righteousness: for he is a babe.

14 But strong meat belongeth to them that are of full age, even those who by reason of use have their senses exercised to discern both good and evil.

There are two realms of the spirit world. The great-unseen world of spirits is divided into the good and evil. Our Lord God and Satan are the rulers over these respective realms. Cherubim, seraphim and angels do the bidding of God. Principalities, powers and rulers of the darkness of this world, wicked spirits in high places, and evil spirits and demons are all under the authority of Satan. These two realms are arrayed against each other, and the war of the ages is still going on. **The Holy Ghost is the active Commander-in-Chief of God's army. He personally indwells and**

energizes spirit-filled believers. Discerning of spirits is a valuable weapon both of defense and offense for the spirit-filled believer.

In the realm of affliction, the Bible speaks of dumb spirits (Matthew 9:21); blind spirits (Matthew 12:22); deaf spirits (Matthew 9:25); spirits of infirmity (Luke 13:11, 16); and spirits of lunacy (Matthew 14:15, 18). There are also cases of those who were just "possessed with devils" (Matthew 4:24).

The gift of discerning of spirits enables the saints of God to approach these cases with knowledge and understanding. With the word of authority, he cast out the evil spirits (Mark 16:17). Paul's reference to seducing spirits and doctrines of devils (1 Timothy 4:1) reveals a very subtle trick of Satan to deceive mankind. Also, in the last days will come false prophets, who will perform miracles with signs and lying wonders in the name of the antichrist (2 Thessalonians 2:9 and Revelations 13:14).

Without the gift of discerning of spirits or discernment, we would not recognize these evil spirits that surrounds us. They dwell on every hand and can only be recognized through the gift of discernment. The Word tells us to know those that labor among us; this can only be done as God reveals to us their true spiritual nature. Not everyone that is evil is possessed of evil spirits, but a good many are. We must be open to the voice of God as He speaks to us concerning those evil spirits. Every spirit-filled believer needs the gift of discernment to fulfill God's calling in his or her life.

Gifts of Power

The Gifts of Power are *Faith, Working of Miracles and Healings.* These gifts operate in the realm of the physical. These are gifts of action, which produce signs and wonders. John states that we shall do the same works as Jesus if we believe.

John 14:10-12

> *[10] Believest thou not that I am in the Father, and the Father in me? the words that I speak unto you I speak not of myself: but the Father that dwelleth in me, he doeth the works. [11] Believe me that I am in the Father, and the Father in me: or else believe me for the very works' sake. [12] Verily, verily, I say unto you, He that believeth on me, the works that I do shall he do also; and greater works than these shall he*

do; because I go unto my Father.

Mark 16:17, 18

17 And these signs shall follow them that be-lieve; In my name shall they cast out devils; they shall speak with new tongues;
18 They shall take up serpents; and if they drink any deadly thing, it shall not hurt them; they shall lay hands on the sick, and they shall recover.

James 5:14, 15

14 Is any sick among you? let him call for the elders of the church; and let them pray over him, anointing him with oil in the name of the Lord:
15 And the prayer of faith shall save the sick, and the Lord shall raise him up; and if he have committed sins, they shall be forgiven him.

1 Corinthians 12:28

And God hath set some in the church, first apostles, secondarily prophets, thirdly teachers, after that miracles, then gifts of healings, helps, governments, diversities of tongues.

Laying hands on the sick, by believers, and anointing with oil by the elders are two ways through which the gifts of healings operate. Healing is the mending of the body when it is sick or diseased. There is also a spiritual healing that takes place when we are spiritually hurt. We call the blind receiving their sight a miracle, but it isn't; it's a healing. Deaf ears unstopped, crooked limbs made straight and cancers disappearing, all this is healing.

One of the greatest modern day preachers who had the gift of healing was Smith Wigglesworth. He tries to teach us in his writings that **to pray the prayer of faith for healing or anything else, we first must get our eyes off the sickness and get our eyes on Jesus.** When our eyes are on Jesus, then we can pray effectively, and God answers our prayer. This is faith in action, and the outcome is to see the hand of God heal or work miracles. But we must keep our eyes upon Jesus.

The Gift of Faith

Faith is the greatest of the gifts of power.

Matthew 17:20

> *And Jesus said unto them, Because of your unbelief: for verily I say unto you, If ye have faith as a grain of mustard seed, ye shall say unto this mountain, Remove hence to yonder place; and it shall remove; and nothing shall be impossible unto you.*

Hebrews 11:3

> *Through faith we understand that the worlds were framed by the word of God, so that things which are seen were not made of things which do appear.*

In the Bible, Hebrews 11:1 defines faith. *"Now faith is the substance of things hoped for, the evidence of things not seen."* To us, faith is believing that something shall be done even though we do not see the results at the time we ask. Yet, we still believe it shall come to pass. **Abraham looked for a city whose builder and maker was God, and by faith, we are still looking for that same city.** By faith, we believe in a resurrected Savior. We have not seen Him with our natural eye, yet we believe He is real and He is alive, and that by faith we shall see Him.

John 15:7

> *If ye abide in me, and my words abide in you, ye shall ask what ye will, and it shall be done unto you.*

Galatians 2:20

> *I am crucified with Christ: nevertheless I live; yet not I, but Christ liveth in me: and the life which I now live in the flesh I live by the faith of the Son of God, who loved me, and gave himself for me.*

Gifts of Miracles

Miracles are an orderly intervention in the regular operations of nature: **a supernatural suspension of natural law.** Elisha made the iron ax head to swim (2 Kings 6:1-7). God turned the sundial of Ahaz 10 degrees backwards (2 Kings 20:11). Aaron cast his rod before Pharaoh and it became a serpent (Exodus 7:10). More examples are when the water in the river was smitten and it became blood, when the water turned into wine, and when Lazarus was raised from the dead; these are miracles.

The Gift of Prophecy

Prophecy is the greatest of the gifts in its class. Prophecy is for the edifying of the church. Prophecy is the foretelling of events that are to take place at some given time in the future.

2 Peter 1:20-21

> *[20] Knowing this first, that no prophecy of the scripture is of any private interpretation.*
> *[21] For the prophecy came not in old time by the will of man: but holy men of God spake as they were moved by the Holy Ghost.*

Exodus 4:12

> *Now therefore go, and I will be with thy mouth, and teach thee what thou shalt say.*

1 Corinthians 14:1-5, 22-32 and 37-40

¹ *Follow after charity, and desire spiritual gifts, but rather that ye may prophesy.*
² *For he that speaketh in an unknown tongue speaketh not unto men, but unto God: for no man understandeth him; howbeit in the spirit he speaketh mysteries.*
³ *But he that prophesieth speaketh unto men to edification, and exhortation, and comfort.*
⁴ *He that speaketh in an unknown tongue edifieth himself; but he that prophesieth edifieth the church.*
⁵ *I would that ye all spake with tongues, but rather that ye prophesied: for greater is he that prophesieth than he that speaketh with tongues, except he interpret, that the church may receive edifying.*
²² *Wherefore tongues are for a sign, not to them that believe, but to them that believe not: but prophesying serveth not for them that believe not, but for them which believe.*
²³ *If therefore the whole church be come together into one place, and all speak with tongues, and there come in those that are unlearned, or unbelievers, will they not say*

that ye are mad?

24 But if all prophesy, and there come in one that believeth not, or one unlearned, he is convinced of all, he is judged of all:

25 And thus are the secrets of his heart made manifest; and so falling down on his face he will worship God, and report that God is in you of a truth.

26 How is it then, brethren? when ye come together, every one of you hath a psalm, hath a doctrine, hath a tongue, hath a revelation, hath an interpretation. Let all things be done unto edifying.

27 If any man speak in an unknown tongue, let it be by two, or at the most by three, and that by course; and let one interpret.

28 But if there be no interpreter, let him keep silence in the church; and let him speak to himself, and to God.

29 Let the prophets speak two or three, and let the other judge.

30 If any thing be revealed to another that sitteth by, let the first hold his peace.

31 For ye may all prophesy one by one, that all may learn, and all may be comforted.

32 And the spirits of the prophets are subject

to the prophets.

[37] If any man think himself to be a prophet, or spiritual, let him acknowledge that the things that I write unto you are the commandments of the Lord.

[38] But if any man be ignorant, let him be ignorant.

[39] Wherefore, brethren, covet to prophesy, and forbid not to speak with tongues.

[40] Let all things be done decently and in order.

The way to tell if a "prophecy" is true is to wait and see if it comes to pass. The word prophesy can be defined as "to speak for God." To prophesy is to yield as the Holy Ghost impresses upon one to speak the message God would have known. It can be a message of condemnation and judgment or of encouragement and hope. Prophecy of events to take place could be as short a time as a few hours or hundreds of years in the future. One important thing to remember: **for prophecy to be truly fulfilled, it must be out of our control to bring it to pass.** Prophecy must be God foretelling events that only He can bring to pass. If prophecies are given, and it's in my or your power to cause its fulfillment, that isn't prophecy. Prophecy deals with the present, sometimes, and the future most all of the time. We must be very careful in judging prophecy.

Tongues and Interpretation

Tongues and Interpretation equals prophecy. In the church today we must have these two gifts in operation. But, **much of the time all that the church concentrates on is tongues and interpretation, when there are seven more gifts of the spirit** that are just as important or more important than tongues and interpretation. One reason for this is because tongues is the physical evidence of the receiving of the baptism of the Holy Ghost.

One of the problems in the Corinthian church was the overuse of the gift of tongues in their services when they came together as a body. Since speaking in tongues is the initial physical evidence of the baptism in the Holy Ghost (as the examples in the book of Acts indicate), it is easy to reach out in faith and claim the gift of tongues.

Because our ear goes out to God as we speak in tongues, and we are blessed and edified, it then becomes easy to respond in tongues every time one feels the moving of the spirit. This meant that in Corinth, tongues were exercised so often in their meetings that the other gifts were neglected. At times, so many would be speaking in tongues that confusion would take over a service.

It's fine to feel the moving of the spirit and speak in tongues. But this does not mean that every person who speaks in tongues is giving a message. **Speaking in tongues edifies the person speaking, just as when we pray in the spirit and speak in tongues in prayer.** It is the Holy Ghost praying to God for our needs and for us.

But a message in tongues is when the Holy Ghost speaks through someone and tells them what He hears straight from the throne of God. **There is a difference in a message from God and someone speaking in tongues.** Most important is that a message be interpreted. Interpretation is when the Holy Ghost begins to deal with your heart to tell the people what He wants them to know. When God first began to deal with me to interpret, I would receive the first few words of the message. I would hold back and ask God, "Lord is this really you, or is it just me?" My heart would race, the spirit would well up inside of me, and I would feel like I would explode. Sometimes I would yield and sometimes not. It's a good thing that the Lord is longsuffering toward us. **All I can say is this, the more we yield, the easier it becomes.** Most of all, do not be afraid to trust God, for he always knows what he is doing. **Our place is to simply be a yielded vessel to be used.** The Word encourages us to pray always. Pray with the mind and heart, and pray in the Holy Ghost, speaking in tongues as the Holy Ghost prays through us.

1 Corinthians 14:14-15

> *[14] For if I pray in an unknown tongue, my spirit prayeth, but my understanding is unfruitful.*
> *[15] What is it then? I will pray with the spirit, and I will pray with the understanding also: I will sing with the spirit, and I will sing with the understanding also."*

Romans 8:26

> *Likewise the Spirit also helpeth our infirmities: for we know not what we should pray for as we ought: but the Spirit itself maketh*

intercession for us with groanings which cannot be uttered.

Let him who has the gift of interpretation consider the importance of his or her gift. **The speaker in tongues is dependent upon the interpreter for the completion of his message.** If the latter fails the message in tongues has been given in vain and the scriptures disobeyed. The responsibility for this failure rests upon the interpreter if he or she has quenched the spirit. Also **the quality of the message in tongues will be judged by the interpretation, for the interpretation is all that is understandable to the hearers.** The message must be for edification, exhortation or to comfort. The spirit-filled Christians that are present will be able to sense whether this has been accomplished.

In Conclusion

I believe that in this study, the material presented clarifies that the Holy Ghost is a person, the third person of the tri-une Godhead. He has feelings as we do. He has been sent by the Father to be our comforter and guide. The Holy Ghost enables our lives by giving to us spiritual gifts as He wills. There are nine primary gifts, each with subdivisions. These gifts He gives severally as He wills. We could have none, one, two, five or all nine. The number given is left up to the Holy Ghost. It is then left up to us to nurture it or them. Be careful to use them wisely and carefully as you are led by the Holy Ghost, so that God's will might be done, praying always.

I hope this study has been a help to you in understanding the Holy Ghost. Also, I hope that you will agree with me that the Holy Ghost is a person and the third person of the trinity. Use this study prayerfully, and ask God what He would have you to discern to be the truth.

The Word tells us to work out our own salvation with fear and trembling. The Holy Ghost is our best friend in this world, and He will stay with us till we go home to be with the Lord. Appreciate Him, welcome Him, love Him, for He is our comforter sent to us by God.

Test Your Knowledge

1. What is the initial physical evidence of the Holy Ghost in a person's life?

_____

_____

2. The Holy Ghost gives gifts to those whom He chooses. How many gifts are there?

_____

3. Name the gifts of the spirit.

_____

_____

_____

_____

4. These gifts are broken down into classes.

Name them.

_____

_____

_____

_____

5. What is the greatest gift in each class?

_____

_____

_____

_____

_____

6. What is discerning of the spirits?

_____

_____

_____

_____

_____

7. Tongues and interpretation equal what?

_____

Have you learned anything from this study?

Editorial Note:

Much prayer before God went into this study, in addition to the following research materials:

The Spirit Himself, by Ralph M. Riggs
Matthew Henry's Commentary on the Whole Bible, by Matthew Henry
The Dake Reference Bible, by Finis Jennings Dake
Thompson Chain Reference Bible

There are other books of study used with a thought or a sentence from here or there, but mostly these. Thanks to the writers without whom this study could not be done.

Test Your Knowledge Answers

Questions on page 21

1. What is the Godhead? 1 John 5:7 *For there are three that bear record in heaven, the Father, the Word, and the Holy Ghost: and these three are one.*

2. How many are in the Godhead and who are they? Three (3)

 God, the Father
 Jesus, the Word, the Son
 Holy Ghost

3. Who shall testify of Jesus? John 15:26 *But when the Comforter is come, whom I will send unto you from the Father, even the Spirit of truth, which proceedeth from the Father, he shall testify of me:*

4. Can we lie to the Holy Ghost? Acts 5:3-4 *[3] But Peter said, Ananias, why hath Satan filled thine heart to lie to the Holy Ghost, and to keep back part of the price of the land? [4] Whiles it remained, was it not thine own? and after it was sold, was it not in thine own power? why hast thou conceived* this thing in thine heart? thou hast not lied unto men, but unto God.

5. How many bear record in Heaven and who are they? 1 John 5:7 *For there are three that bear record in Heaven, the Father, the Word, and the Holy Ghost: and these three are one.*

6. What formula did Jesus give for water baptism? Matthew 28:18-19 *[18]And Jesus came and spake unto them, saying, All power is given unto me in heaven and in earth. [19] Go ye therefore, and teach all nations, baptizing them in the name of the Father, and of the Son, and of the Holy Ghost:*

Questions on page 43

1. What does the Word tell us to covet? 1 Corinthians 12:31 *But covet earnestly the best gifts: and yet shew I unto you a more excellent way.*

2. Who is the Comforter? Acts 9:31 *Then had the churches rest throughout all Judaea and Galilee and Samaria, and were edified; and walking in the fear of the Lord, and in the comfort of the Holy Ghost, were multiplied.*

3. How does the Holy Ghost help our infirmities? Romans 8:26 *Likewise the spirit also helpeth our infirmities: for we know not what we should pray for as we ought: but the Spirit itself maketh intercession for us with groanings which cannot be uttered.*

4. What is the blasphemy against the Holy Ghost? Blasphemy against the Holy Ghost, in my opinion and according to scripture, is this: After a person has been enlightened, has tasted of the heavenly gift, and has been made a partaker of the Holy Ghost, if they deny the reality of their experiences, they have committed blasphemy. These are people who know what it is to be saved and set free from sin, to be filled with the Holy Ghost and feel the very presence of God. If, knowing all that has happened to them, they turn their backs on God and publicly deny all they have experienced, saying, "God is not real; the Holy Ghost baptism isn't real. It's all lies," is blasphemy against the Holy Ghost and will never be forgiven in this world, neither will it be forgiven in the world to come.

5. What will the Holy Ghost reprove the world of? John 16:8 *And when he is come, he will* *reprove the world of sin, and of righteousness, and of judgment:*

6. What is sanctification, and why is it so important in the life of a Christian? It is the separation of ourselves from sin, the laying aside or laying down of those things which entangle us in the world.

Questions on page 75

1. What is the difference between personality and corporeity?
Personality (being a person)
Corporeity (having a body)

2. What does the Holy Ghost do in the conversion of sinners? Convict us of sin

3. What is the baptism of the Holy Ghost, and how does it differ from salvation? Salvation is when Jesus comes into our hearts to dwell. (We changed from the old man of sin into a new creature.) The baptism of the Holy Ghost is when we invite, through prayer, the Holy Ghost to come into our lives and hearts.

4. Name the symbols of the Holy Ghost? To name a few: Oil, Wind, Water, Dove

5. List four important things that the Holy Ghost does? Any of the following: convicts people of their sins; gives courage; gives power from on high; comforts; guides; instructs; gives wisdom

Questions on page 141

1. What is the initial physical evidence of the Holy Ghost in a person's life? Acts 2:4 *And they were all filled with the Holy Ghost, and began to speak with other tongues as the Spirit gave them utterance.*

2. The Holy Ghost gives gifts to those whom He chooses; how many gifts are there? Nine (9)

3. Name them.
      The Word of Wisdom
      The Word of Knowledge
      Discerning of Spirits
      The Gift of Healings
      The Gift of Faith
      The Gift of Miracles
      The Gift of Prophecy

The Gift of Tongues
The Gift of Interpretation

4. These gifts are broken down into classes. Name them.
Gifts of Revelation
Gifts of Power
Gifts of Utterance

5. What is the greatest gift in each class?
In the gifts of Revelation: **Word of Wisdom**
In the gifts of Power: **Faith**
In the gifts of Utterance: **Prophecy**

6. What is discerning of the spirits?
Without the gift of discerning of spirits or discernment, we would not recognize evil spirits that surround us. The gift of discerning of spirits enables the saints of God to approach these cases with knowledge and understanding.

7. Tongues and interpretation equal what?
Prophecy

— Notes —

— Notes —

— Notes —

— Notes —

Coming Soon!

Look for Rev. Wilson's upcoming study on *The Three Johns* through **Paradise Gospel Press** and **Amazon**. Enjoy the following excerpt from the book:

Chapter 1

1 John 1:1

> *That which was from the beginning, which we have heard, which we have seen with our eyes, which we have looked upon, and our hands have handled, of the Word of life;*

The book of Saint John starts where all narratives should start: in the beginning. Saint John 1:1 tells us: *"In the beginning was the Word, and the Word was with God, and the Word was God."* John is making it plain that Jesus was there when the world was created, that He was involved in the creation work, and that Jesus is God (the Son of God) and He and His Father are one. Some people have a problem with the fact that Jesus was man and God at the same time. They ask, was He God or was He man? They don't seem to be able to understand that Jesus was God in a man's body. If we look at His birth, we see that Mary was a virgin, that the Holy Ghost moved within her and she became with child. The child's Father was God. This child, like all children, was born of His mother's womb. Like all children, He had to learn to crawl before He could walk and run. The difference was in His loving nature, because He knew who He was and what He came to earth to do.

At the age of twelve, He was found in the temple sitting amid the doctors asking questions, and they "were astonished at his understanding and answers." About the age of thirty, He began His ministry with signs and wonders following, then at the end of three-and-a-half years of preaching and healing the sick, Jesus was crucified on a cross for the sins of the whole world. After His death and resurrection, the disciples began to preach the gospel of Jesus Christ; and the church came into being and began to grow and spread.

All of this brings us to the first Epistle of John and why he wrote it. John was worried about the church, because false teachings were coming in. These false teachings were leading people away from the truth of God's Word. At this time, John was a very old man, but he felt that he had to do something. So, his only option was to write letters to remind these saints of the importance of staying true to the word of God and what they had been taught from the beginning, lest there come in those who would lead them away unto falsehoods, teaching the doctrines of men. Satan is a very serious enemy; his goal is to destroy the church of the Living God. One thing we must remember is that for everything God has, the devil has a counterfeit. Scripture tells us that there will come in those who have a form of godliness but deny the power thereof and from such to turn away.

You will want your own copy of this exciting new study coming Summer 2017 at www.ParadiseGospelPress.com.

www.ingramcontent.com/pod-product-compliance
Lightning Source LLC
Chambersburg PA
CBHW060900280326
41934CB00007B/1121